MW01171882

PERSONAL REVIVAL

Yearning for the Kingdom of God

PAUL JINADU

Copyright © 2022 by Paul Jinadu

ISBN 9798352376577
All rights reserved.

New Covenant Church
Nigeria National Administrative Office
P.M.B. 5450, Dugbe
Ibadan, Nigeria
www.newcovenantchurchnigeria.org

New Covenant Church Logistics
9606 East Foothill Blvd.
Rancho Cucamonga, CA 91730 (909) 791-8095
http://www.nccworld.org/
info@nccworld.org

All Scripture, unless otherwise stated, are taken from
the New King James Version of the Bible. Scriptures
marked "NIV" are taken from the Holy Bible, New
International Version®, NIV®. Copyright © 1973,
1978, 1984, 2011 by Biblica, Inc.™ Used by
permission of Zondervan.
Scripture quotations taken from the (NASB®) New
American Standard Bible®, Copyright © 1960, 1971,
1977, 1995, 2020 by The Lockman Foundation. Used
by permission. All rights reserved.
www.lockman.org.

Contents

Contents (Continued)

Preface

We normally associate revival with times when the Holy Spirit visits a church or community, a town, a city, or a country. It usually starts small among a praying people. Once the fire falls on that group, it quickly spreads to surrounding areas. Other times, a visitor can catch the fire and take it miles away back to his or her community. It involves a longing for true worship, a desire to witness to non-believers, and deep conviction and confession of sins. Generally, church attendance explodes to the upside. Lives of individual believers are transformed and there is a ripple effect upon the general public.

Historically, Holy Spirit revivals do not happen frequently. For example, the last visitation in South Wales, UK was in 1904, in Lowestoft, England in 1921 and in the Hebrides, Scotland in 1949. Personal revival, on the other hand, is different. It happens all the time. It is more predictable because the individual carries the responsibility to start one.

In this book we will use the life of Peter the Apostle as our guide. What God did for him and through him happened because he went through certain processes. All we need to do is to simply follow in his footsteps.

Introduction

When the day of Pentecost came, they were all together in one place. Suddenly a sound like the blowing of a violent wind came from heaven and filled the whole house where they were sitting. They saw what seemed to be tongues of fire that separated and came to rest on each of them. All of them were filled with the Holy Spirit and began to speak in other tongues as the Spirit enabled them (Acts 2:1-4).

When the fire of the Holy Spirit falls on a person he becomes transformed from the inside out. It is the greatest miracle God can perform in a man, second only to the miracle of the new birth. Since the day of Pentecost, the world has changed for good. God has begun to live among men, redeeming them, empowering them, and living in intimate fellowship with them (unlike the Old Testament times when God was more remote).

Hebrews 12:18-21 says, *You have not come to a mountain that can be touched and that is burning with fire; to darkness, gloom and storm; to a trumpet blast or to such a voice speaking words that those who heard it begged that no further word be spoken to them, because they could not bear what was commanded: "If even an animal touches the mountain, it must be stoned to death." The sight was so terrifying that Moses said, "I am trembling with fear."*

There was something unique about the Pentecostal experience for the disciples who gathered in the Upper Room, and in particular the Apostle Peter. After they left that room in less than an hour Jerusalem had felt the impact. On that day about 3% of the population of Jerusalem turned to the Lord. Just a few weeks or months later the church population had swelled to about 8% of Jerusalem, something we don't often see today. The household of Cornelius also received the Holy Spirit.

As I began to speak, the Holy Spirit came on them as he had come on us at the beginning. Then I remembered what the Lord had said: "John baptised with water, but you will be baptised with the Holy Spirit." So if God gave them the same gift he gave us who believed in the Lord Jesus Christ, who was I to think that I could stand in God's way? (Acts 11:15-17)

Peter clearly affirmed that the Holy Spirit came upon the people gathered at Cornelius' house, just as He had come upon them in the Upper Room. What was the evidence Peter produced to convince the people who questioned his visit to the home of a Gentile?

While Peter was still speaking these words, the Holy Spirit came on all who heard the message. The circumcised believers who had come with Peter were astonished that the gift of the Holy Spirit had been poured out even on Gentiles. For they heard them speaking in tongues and praising God (Acts 10:44-46).

Speaking in tongues was what Peter and Cornelius had in common when the Holy Spirit came upon them. There is no record, however, that the household of Cornelius went out to do exploits like the apostles who emerged from the Upper Room. The clue to that puzzle can only be found in the way God had prepared the disciples who followed Jesus for three and a half years. Without this preparation, the apostles (and the disciples who followed in their footsteps) would only have a claim to be Pentecostals because they spoke in tongues and exercised some other spiritual gifts.

What made Peter not only to be baptised in the Holy Spirit but be filled with the Holy Spirit after Pentecost is the thrust of this book. I firmly believe that if the millions of people who speak in tongues today had an encounter with the Holy Spirit as Peter and the other disciples did, the church and the world would not be in the sorry state we see today. The experience of Peter from Gethsemane to the Upper Room will give us insight.

Chapter One
THREE PHASES IN THE LIFE OF PETER

From the arrest of Jesus right up to the coming of the Holy Spirit at Pentecost Peter had experiences that set him apart from the rest of the apostles. These are experiences we all need to pass through if we are serious about experiencing personal revival. Peter happened to be around three fires when he had each of these experiences. We have The Fire of Self-Revelation, The Fire of Restoration, and The Fire of Personal Revival at Pentecost.

Peter, in common with the rest of the disciples, was not saved until after Calvary. They were hoping for the coming of the Redeemer by following the Levitical requirements. Like their master, Jesus, they were fully observant Jews. After the Cross, however—the price for our redemption having been paid—the disciples could now look back with assurance of faith in the finished work of Christ.

What the average believer has in common with Peter is the third of the three fires, the fire of Pentecost. However, our experience of the power of the Holy Spirit will not be at the same level as that of Peter unless we too pass through similar encounters Peter had around the other two fires. The Lord must deal with us after Pentecost the same way He dealt with Peter before Pentecost in order for us to become world changers like him.

So, what happened to Peter in the Upper Room that turned him into a human dynamo may appear instantaneous; but it was actually the end of a long process. Without the fire of self-revelation, and the fire of restoration, the fire of Pentecost would not have turned into a personal revival that totally transformed Peter into a dynamic world changer, a man the Holy Spirit found easy to move through.

Chapter Two
WHY COULDN'T WE CAST IT OUT?

I don't know about you, but I had some serious questions as a young believer. Reading the Gospels and the Book of Acts gave me a clear insight into what God was capable of doing, willing to do, and is most certainly ready and eager to continue to do them today. I was asking questions similar to Gideon's:

> *The angel of the Lord came and sat down under the oak in Ophrah that belonged to Joash the Abiezrite, where his son Gideon was threshing wheat in a winepress to keep it from the Midianites. When the angel of the Lord appeared to Gideon, he said, "The Lord is with you, mighty warrior." "Pardon me, my lord,"* Gideon replied, *"but if the Lord is with us, why has all this happened to us? Where are all his wonders that our ancestors told us about when they said, 'Did not the Lord bring us up out of Egypt?' But now the Lord has abandoned us and given us into the hand of Midian"* (Judges 6:11-13).

I was desperate for the days of Elijah to come again, for us to see the move of God as was commonplace in the Early Church. I had a good reason for asking all these questions. The questions were mostly in my head because I didn't think anyone around me knew the answers. If they did, I reckoned they would have found the answers and be doing exploits in the name of the Lord long time before I was saved. Then churches would be true Pentecostal churches.

Those were the days of "tarrying," when Christians would sit down in meetings, patiently waiting for the Holy Spirit to "fall" on them as on the Day of Pentecost. So, I reasoned that we weren't seeing a continuation of the Acts because the majority of people in church—even Pentecostal churches in those days—were still waiting for the baptism of the Holy Spirit.

My Experience at Conversion

It was a miraculous encounter in Chelmsford, Essex, England in 1961 that led to my conversion to Christ. You could say I started at the top and there was no going back.

I was born a Muslim, but I wasn't brought up a Muslim. By that I mean I had little or no encouragement to follow the Islamic faith, even though my family were Muslims. Both my parents were Muslims only in name. For me, it was like I was born to be a Muslim. I didn't need any encouragement at all to worship Allah. Fortunately for me I didn't have far to go to attend a mosque. There was one right opposite our house. I used to attend the prayers all by myself. I even enrolled myself into a nearby Koranic school, so eager was I to immerse in the religion.

I didn't need to be told to observe some of the rules of the religion, one of which was total abstinence from alcohol. Indeed, I was so close-minded that it never occurred to me that anyone could change sides and become a Christian convert. Up until my conversion, I only ever heard of Christians who converted to Islam; not the other way around.

I was sent to an Anglican primary school, and Bible Knowledge was actually my best subject. On relocating to the UK in 1957 to complete my secondary school education, I took up lodgings with a Christian family in Norbury, South London. They were staunch Methodists and insisted I attend church services with them; which I did. I didn't really care whether I attended a Christian school or lived in a vicarage. I was so committed to Islam I knew nobody and nothing could shake my faith.

My world was turned upside down, however, in November 1961 when in Chelmsford, Essex, Jesus met with me. I was in Chelmsford preparing for my A levels with a view to going to medical school. A fellow student took a particular interest in becoming my friend. Unknown to me, he was a vibrant believer. This was friendship evangelism. At every opportunity he would invite me to Christian programmes, but I never showed interest. I must have been a very hard nut to crack.

I was silent about my faith, but resolute. I didn't agree or disagree about any discussions about religion. I was just immovable. The poor fellow must have been tearing his hair out trying to figure out the best angle to introduce Christ to me.

One day he succeeded to arouse my interest in this particular gospel outreach at the City Hall in Chelmsford. To cut a long story short, God met with me at that meeting. I had my own Damascus Road experience. Jesus literally appeared to me and asked me to follow Him.

The events of the previous fifteen minutes had prepared me for this encounter with the risen Lord. After presenting a simple gospel message, the Evangelist closed with these statements: "I don't want you to believe in a dead Christ. If Jesus died for our sins and on the third day rose again, then He must be alive. Not only is He alive, but He is here, according to the Bible." He continued: "And if He is here, we can expect Him to do the same miracles today as He did in Bible days."

The preacher had my attention now. They say seeing is believing and this man was going to persuade Jesus to prove Himself alive. He didn't try to convince the audience about which religion is the best or what is the right way to heaven. He stood on the platform of Jesus proving Himself to us. By performing miracles before our very eyes, Jesus would show that He was alive. If He was alive, then it will prove that truly His death on the cross was effective in washing away our sins.

I was ever so eager to see Jesus show up in Chelmsford; and show up He did that night. The Evangelist Peter Scothern called out for people who needed a miracle because their cases were beyond medical intervention. He prayed for many people, but only two instances stood out to me. One was a deaf lady who got her earing back instantaneously. The second was a lady with one leg that was shorter than the other. The lady was healed right before my incredulous eyes. I was in the front row: I witnessed everything.

Then Jesus Came

Some huge immovable object was dislodged in my heart by those miracles. I had witnessed a phenomenon; something science couldn't explain. I knew there was power in the room. I was impressed, but not yet fully convinced. Then came the biggest miracle of the night. Jesus appeared to me in a flash. He looked into my eyes and I felt His love. It was like meeting someone for the first time, and yet it felt like you've known them all your life.

That night I gave my heart to Christ and became a born-again Christian.

Compassion For the Lost

If a staunch, almost fanatical Muslim like me can be saved after hearing the gospel for the first time through someone anointed enough to preach the gospel "with the Holy Spirit sent down from heaven," then there is hope for the rest of us. From that night my quest for the power of God to manifest in my life began.

After His suffering, He presented Himself to them and gave many convincing proofs that He was alive" (Acts 1:3).

I wanted to be able, just like the evangelist, to get Jesus to give *many convincing proofs that He was alive.*

As I was reading through the Bible one day this text leapt out of the pages and hit me right between the eyes, as it were:

But you will receive power when the Holy Spirit comes on you; and you will be my witnesses in Jerusalem, and in all Judea and Samaria, and to the ends of the earth (Acts 1:8).

"That's it," I concluded. "The answer to my quest: the baptism of the Holy Spirit. That must be the secret of the powerful anointing manifesting in the life of that evangelist." So, I set out to look for that wonderful experience.

Come, Holy Spirit

Within four months I had been baptised in water and had received the baptism of the Holy Spirit with the evidence of speaking in tongues. A glorious experience it was, but Pentecost it was not. I had the gifts and the sensations and the goosebumps, but I wasn't "turning the world upside down" like the apostles. Years went by before I came to realize that something was missing. I was expecting to mimic the experiences of the apostles after their Upper Room visitation, but I didn't even come close. This may not be everyone's experiences, but it was certainly mine. I had the liberty of the Spirit in prayer and worship. I felt closer to the Lord in my daily walk, and my love of reading the Word rose sharply, but that was about it.

This reminded me of the cry of the frustrated disciples: "Why could we not cast it out?" (Matthew 17:19) As I continued to study the Word and also read about experiences of great men of God past and present, I got the picture. The Day of Pentecost was the culmination of months and years of God's dealings with the disciples. By the end of the ten days wait in the Upper Room, they were ready. No wonder Acts 2:1 says, *"When the Day of Pentecost had fully come, they were all with one accord in one place."*

I was very eager to get to the bottom of this mystery: why we don't often see the same level of Holy Spirit activity after being baptised in the Holy Spirit as on the Day of Pentecost? While I was grateful to the Lord for saving me, I was also deeply moved with compassion for lost humanity, especially my fellow Muslims. It was at this time during the early months of my newfound faith in Christ that I had a call to the ministry to preach the gospel to everyone.

What struck me and drove me to immediate surrender was the word of the Lord to me: "If you, too, can preach the gospel with evidence so that people will know that I am alive and ready to do the same things today as I did in Bible days, even strict Muslims will give Me their hearts." That rung a bell with me. I doubt if I would have surrendered my life to Christ if He hadn't proved Himself to be alive and the same right before my eyes. Everybody deserves the same chance to believe. Amen?

So, I needed to find out why what was common occurrences in the first century church was happening less frequently in our time, and the answer was not difficult to find. The disciples met certain conditions before Pentecost which made revival to break out spontaneously in the Upper Room. If anyone could meet the same or similar conditions after their encounter with the Holy Spirit, he or she should see similar results.

No one epitomises these conditions better than Peter. By the time the Day of Pentecost came, Peter and the other eleven disciples of Jesus were primed and ready for the dynamic demonstration of the power of God. As Peter said in Acts 3:10-13,

While the man held on to Peter and John, all the people were astonished and came running to them in the place called Solomon's Colonnade. When Peter saw this, he said to them: "Fellow Israelites, why does this surprise you? Why do you stare at us as if by

our own power or godliness we had made this man walk? The God of Abraham, Isaac and Jacob, the God of our fathers, has glorified his servant Jesus."

These were ordinary men endowed with the extraordinary power of God. God was able to move through them unhindered. In Peter's experience around three fires we see clearly how God, who prepared him for the encounter with the Holy Spirit at Pentecost, can prepare us too. The only difference is, what Peter went through before Pentecost we need to go through after the baptism of the Holy Spirit for maximum impact. What took Peter three years took me from 1962 to 1967 before I began to see the fulness of the Spirit mature into a great anointing of the Holy Spirit. I was then able to preach the gospel with the Holy Spirit sent down from heaven.

Chapter Three
THE FIRE OF SELF-REVELATION

Now we come to the three fires in the life of Peter. These are life-changing events that happened to Peter around a fire; a literal fire on two occasions and then the fire of the Holy Spirit at Pentecost.

Luke 22:54-58 says, *Having arrested Him, they led Him and brought Him into the high priest's house. But Peter followed at a distance. 55 Now when they had kindled a fire in the midst of the courtyard and sat down together, Peter sat among them. And a certain servant girl, seeing him as he sat by the fire, looked intently at him and said, "This man was also with Him." But he denied Him, saying, "Woman, I do not know Him."*

This event which took place in the courtyard of the High Priest's house, while Peter and others stood around the fire to warm themselves, would be etched permanently in his memory. Three times Peter was challenged about his association with the "accused", the Lord Jesus. Three times Peter denied knowing Him. Why the change of heart? For three and a half years Peter had gladly and openly identified with Jesus in the sight of everyone. Why should he deny Him now?

Peter's reactions were all the more unexpected, seeing how vehemently he had pledged to stand by Jesus come what may. *He said to Him, "Lord, I am ready to go with You, both to prison and to death"* (Luke 22:33).

Peter meant it. He was sold out to Jesus and His cause. He had left everything to follow this Man from Galilee, and there was no going back.

Divine Revelation

Peter was no casual follower of Christ. He was called by Jesus and in obedience, he left his fishing business and followed Him. Later his commitment was endorsed by God's confirmation about Jesus.

> *He said to them, "But who do you say that I am?" Simon Peter answered and said, "You are the Christ, the Son of the living God." Jesus answered and said to him, "Blessed are you, Simon Bar-Jonah, for flesh and blood has not revealed this to you, but My Father who is in heaven. And I also say to you that you are Peter, and on this rock I will build My church, and the gates of Hades shall not prevail against it." (Matthew 16:15-18).*

In a way he was the lead disciple, and on many occasions, he was the chief spokesperson for the twelve. We are talking about a totally committed follower. So, what happened?

Jesus had warned him that he would fail his Master at the crucial hour. *"Then He said, "I tell you, Peter, the rooster shall not crow this day before you will deny three times that you know Me"* (Luke 22:34).

Clearly Peter had the Word, for Jesus plainly foretold his failing. *Peter said to Him, "Even if I have to die with You, I will not deny You!" And so said all the disciples"* (Matt 26:35). It is interesting what Peter was implying here by his response to this prediction by Jesus.

Jesus gave the Word: *"Peter, you are going to deny knowing Me three times."* Peter disagreed with the Word coming from the Man he had been inspired to call: *"You are the Messiah, the Son of the living God."* He was so sure of himself that he dared to contradict the Word of God.

Telling God What to Do

Not only was Peter sure of himself and his loyalty to Christ, but he also thought he knew what God should do.

Matthew 16:21-23 says, *From that time on Jesus began to explain to his disciples that he must go to Jerusalem and suffer many things at the hands of the elders, the chief priests and the teachers of the law, and that he must be killed and on the third day be raised to life. Peter took him aside and began to rebuke him.*

"Never, Lord!" he said. "This shall never happen to you!" Jesus turned and said to Peter, "Get behind me, Satan! You are a stumbling-block to me; you do not have in mind the concerns of God, but merely human concerns."

Something was going on in Peter's heart too deep for he himself to fathom. Peter was following a Messiah of his own making. The suffering Servant was an alien thought to him. His was a conquering Messiah whose kingdom on earth had come. He was glad to be a part of it, and to this end he was prepared to follow Jesus to the bitter end. However, Peter had a problem with the Cross.

The Offense of the Cross

Brothers and sisters, if I am still preaching circumcision, why am I still being persecuted? In that case the offence of the cross has been abolished (Galatians 5:11).

The offense of the Cross is not just the fact that Jesus died on the cross, but that it cuts to the root of human merit in the matter of justification, whether in the form of legal observance, holy dispositions, or good works. The Jews accused Stephen not of worshipping or preaching Christ crucified, but of speaking against the law and the holy place. Paul could have avoided persecution if he preached that

Christ's death on the cross was only an example to us of humility and submission, but he preached righteousness by the cross alone through faith. And it was because of this the Pharisees were offended.

Peter was so keen to demonstrate to the Lord— and indeed to the rest of his fellow apostles—that he was strong and zealous. Christ on the Cross would negate all Peter believed in: human effort.

An Inadequate Self-Image

At this point all that Peter knew about himself was a sum total of his life experiences. He didn't realise he didn't know all there was to know about himself until he saw it in the face of Jesus.

Most Christians never grow beyond a certain point in their walk with God. They may gain a deep knowledge of God through personal study and good solid Biblical teaching in church. Knowledge of God is not the same as an experience of God. I am not talking about an experience from God. We all have those from time to time. To have an experience of God is to meet God, the Holy Spirit. He doesn't at this time give you gifts, anointing, or revelation. He comes to give Himself. It's an exchange.

Isaiah 40:31 says, *But those who wait on the Lord shall renew their strength; they shall mount up with wings like eagles, they shall run and not be weary, they shall walk and not faint.*

This renewal is more akin to an exchange: my weakness for His strength. For Peter to do the exchange, he had to discover himself first; or more appropriately, his self-life had to be revealed to him. If we too want to get deeper with God, our self-life also has to be revealed to us.

Chapter Four
THE LOOK THAT CHANGED PETER

But Peter said, "Man, I do not know what you are saying!" Immediately, while he was still speaking, the rooster crowed. And the Lord turned and looked at Peter. Then Peter remembered the word of the Lord, how He had said to him, "Before the rooster crows, you will deny Me three times." So Peter went out and wept bitterly" (Luke 22:60-62).

Someone must have opened the door to the interrogation room where Jesus was being held. Peter had stood by the fire all night, ashamed of Jesus, yet committed to Him. Three times in the small hours of the morning Peter had been challenged, and three times he vehemently—even using strong language—denied he was ever acquainted with Jesus. It is incredible that Peter of all people would go against everything he believed in for the past three and a half years. He was probably in shock. At this point the Word Jesus had spoken to him was not registering at all.

While denying knowing Jesus, Peter's gaze was nevertheless fixated on that door to the interrogation room. For a moment, Peter ignored his accusers and looked longingly towards that door that was now opening. Maybe it had opened before daybreak, as people were coming and going, but only Jesus' back was visible. Peter was hoping against hope to catch a glimpse of Jesus. On the dot, the cock crowed soon after Peter's third denial. Simultaneously as the door opened, Jesus turned and looked at Peter. Their eyes connected and Peter was brought face to face with his inner self by the piercing gaze of Jesus.

The Face: Reminder of the Word

It took just one look for Peter to be jolted back into reality, as if he had been sleep-walking all his life. Peter remembered the Words of Jesus: *"Before the cock crows you will deny knowing Me three times."* The scales fell off Peter's inner eyes. For the first time in his life Peter realised God knew him better than he knew himself.

Self-revelation needs only to happen to us once in a lifetime. It knocks a man off his pedestal. We know about sins, about habits, about relationships, good or awkward ones. What we don't know, and so many never discover this in a lifetime, is self. The Word of God and a look into the face of Jesus are like miracle mirrors.

Until you know yourself, you cannot surrender yourself, because you won't know what to give away. It is when we have discovered ourselves that the exchange with the Holy Spirit can take place. If I don't know what I am giving away, I may unknowingly take it back. This revelation of self is what prepares the believer for the fulness of the Holy Spirit. This process can take many years for some. For others it may never take place if no one tells them it's there for the taking. Some call it total sanctification, while others prefer to call it full surrender.

I'll never forget the day the Holy Spirit met with me at this level. I was saved, baptised in water, and baptised in the Holy Spirit with the evidence of speaking in tongues. I thought that was it. I was set. I read my Bible copiously, prayed almost continually, spoke in tongues throughout the day, fasted regularly, answered the call to full-time ministry, and now was training to be a minister of the gospel. "What more was there?" I thought.

Then I met some godly men and women. They were all from different backgrounds and doing a variety of jobs, like doctors, nurses, teachers, carpenters, and bakers. They were like the Ark of the Covenant: carriers of the glory of God. My local church in Chelmsford brought in some powerful men of God to speak to us on special occasions, like Easter weekends. I was exposed to the ministry of some highly anointed servants of God whose faith moved mountains of life's challenges and disabilities right before our eyes.

The people I met in The Bible College of Wales, Swansea, founded by Rees Howells, were different. On the whole, they were not outstanding in their gifting, but there was something they had in common. They radiated God. You have to see it to know what I'm talking about. Looking at them, working alongside them in the Bible College's daily chores, I was able to observe each of them at close quarters. They created that hunger in me for a deeper walk with the Holy Spirit. It took me nearly a year of searching before I found the secret. "I must decrease, and He must increase" (John 3:30). Obviously, when the Holy Spirit increases in a person, He becomes more prominent in all they do and how they react to situations. Duncan Campbell used to call it: *"God in dungarees."* In other words, ordinary men and women, doing ordinary jobs, but filled with our extraordinary God.

Chapter Five
MEN WHO WERE ALSO TRANSFORMED

There were other men in the Bible who were similarly transformed like Peter when they saw the Lord.

Job Saw Him

Job 42:5-6 says, *"My ears had heard of you but now my eyes have seen you. Therefore I despise myself and repent in dust and ashes."*

In the midst of his troubles, Job could still cling on to his plea of innocence. He knew he'd done nothing to deserve all the awful things that befell him. If ever he had the chance to speak to God face to face, he would plead his case and demand an explanation. To him, it was unfair that the righteous should suffer in the way he was suffering.

Then one day God showed up: face to face with Job. He was speechless. One look at God's face, whichever form that took, was life changing. Through the Word, Job knew God and tried to please Him as best as he could. What happened when he looked into God's face also happened to Peter and to everyone who looks into that face throughout the ages.

When Job looked at God, he saw himself.

Let the Word Study You

While it is possible to gaze into the face of Jesus in a special time of visitation, looking into Jesus' face to see our self-reflection can happen in a much less dramatic way. I have waited on Him for hours per day in anticipation of catching a glimpse of His face. Yes, I have seen that face, and saw my self-life reflected back. I have wept bitterly like Peter as I saw how corrupt I was by comparison with His crystal glass purity. Actually, it wasn't my sins that disturbed me so much as my self-righteousness. I suddenly realised God wasn't interested in my self-efforts at all. Just as salvation is by grace through faith, so is sanctification.

What has had a greater and more lasting transformational impact on me is the Word. Finding Jesus in His Word; seeing the living Word in the written Word.

> *Do not merely listen to the word, and so deceive yourselves. Do what it says. Anyone who listens to the word but does not do what it says is like someone who looks at his face in a mirror and, after looking at himself, goes away and immediately forgets what he looks like. But whoever looks intently into the perfect law that gives freedom and continues in it—not forgetting what they have heard but doing it— they will be blessed in what they do"* (James 1:22-25).

It is one thing to study the Word of God. It is another thing to let the Word study you. To do this I imagine that the Bible is God's letter to me. I believe that He would have written it even if I were the only believer in the whole world at any given time.

From July to December of 1964, after graduating from the Bible College of Wales, I returned to my home church in Chelmsford, Essex, and rented a room with some members of the church. For six months, after formal studies for two years in Wales, I went to the public library every day (except Sunday) to read the Bible. I was speed reading it so I could get a full picture of the whole Bible. In that time, I read the Bible from cover to cover about twelve times. I read it in different versions. To break the monotony, I frequently went into the Cathedral in the city centre to pray. On average, I spent about six hours a day reading the Bible in addition to my normal devotional times.

Those were life transforming days and months. Each day that I read the Bible it was like God was painting a picture of the face of Jesus on the canvas of my heart. I began to see the Bible as the Word of God, both written and living. Gradually as I saw His face, I also saw my heart, my fallen self.

Those pictures of Jesus' face and of the Holy Spirit have stayed with me ever since. Each time I pray, I get a distinct picture of which member of the Godhead I am addressing. These pictures are more like an impression on the canvas of my mind. I seem to know something I cannot put into words.

Jesus Within Revealed

But when God, who set me apart from my mother's womb and called me by his grace, was pleased to reveal his Son in me so that I might preach him among the Gentiles, my immediate response was not to consult any human being (Galatians 1:15-16 NIV).

This text is the great mystery of the transformation of the believer. Something wonderful happened to Paul in his Damascus Road encounter. God revealed Jesus to him. This led to his dramatic conversion by the roadside. However, something much deeper happened in Paul probably later. God was pleased "to reveal his Son" in him. This is conversion followed by transformation, without which no believer can ever become the person God designed him or her to be.

We cannot be like Christ by keeping His commandments. Neither can we copy His lifestyle and model ourselves on Him. It is virtually impossible to completely mimic another person, let alone the divine nature of the Son of God. Even if we could mimic His behaviour, we cannot copy His intentions or motivations. It is impossible to be like Christ unless Christ Himself lives His own life in and through us.

That was why Jesus was revealed in Paul. Not so that Paul can copy this internal image, but so he can acknowledge that it is not possible. He would then submit to the work of the Holy Spirit, the Spirit of truth (reality), who alone can make Jesus manifest in us.

As Rees Howells put it: "To receive Christ as Saviour you give up your sin. To receive the Holy Spirit as Comforter, you give up yourself. It is easier to give up sin than it is to give up self."

Rees Howells Recounts His Encounter with the Holy Spirit

"It was unconditional surrender." Rees cried his heart out, because, as he said, "I had received a sentence of death, as really as a prisoner in the dock. I had lived in my body for twenty-six years, and could I easily give it up? Who could give his life up to another person in an hour? Why does a man struggle when death comes if it is easy to die? I knew that the only place fit for the old nature was on the cross. Paul makes that very plain in Romans 6. But once this is done in reality, it is done for ever. I could not run into this. I intended to do it, but oh, the cost! I wept for days. I lost seven pounds in weight, just because I saw what He was offering me."

"How I wished I had never seen it! One thing He reminded me of was that He had only come to take what I had already promised the Saviour, not in part, but the whole. Since He died for me, I had died in Him, and I knew that the new life was His and not mine. That had been clear in my mind for three years. So, He had only come to take what was his own. I saw that only the Holy Ghost in me could live like the Saviour. Everything He told me appealed to me; it was only a question of the loss there would be in doing it. I didn't give my answer in a moment, and He didn't want me to. It took five days to make the decision, days which were spent alone with God."

There are certain experiences in life that only come as one is willing to spend time alone with God. Often, very few of these transactions are done in public. Responding to altar calls and receiving ministry in meetings is a good place to start a move towards God. Real encounters, however, often take place when one is alone. That's the place where you can really count the cost and not say words you don't mean or make pledges you can't keep. Remember Jesus at the Garden of Gethsemane: He "went a little farther" (Matthew 26:39). Even His most trusted disciples could not join Him there. That is why I believe there must have been a gap between the time when God revealed Jesus to Paul and when He revealed Jesus *in him*. It was total exchange, which can be very costly to the flesh.

As with Isaiah, so with Rees Howells

In the year that King Uzziah died, I saw the Lord sitting on a throne, high and lifted up, and the train of His robe filled the temple (Isaiah 6:1).

Seeing the Lord is like a two-edged sword. You cannot see the Lord and not see yourself. We see a reflection of our old self on His face. When you see someone who is full of himself and judges and criticises a fellow believer, you can tell immediately he hasn't seen the Lord. This was the experience of Isaiah:

So I said: "Woe is me, for I am undone! Because I am a man of unclean lips, and I dwell in the midst of a people of unclean lips; for my eyes have seen the King, the Lord of hosts" (Isaiah 6:5).

Like Isaiah, Rees Howells saw the holiness of God. He said, "and seeing Him, I saw my own corrupt nature. It wasn't sins that I saw, but nature touched by the fall. I was corrupt to the core. I knew I had to be cleansed; I saw there was as much difference between the Holy Ghost and myself as between light and darkness."

"Nothing is more real to me than the process I went through for that whole week," he continued. "The Holy Spirit went on dealing with me, exposing the root of my nature which was self. Sin was cancelled, and it wasn't sin He was dealing with; it was self—that thing which came from the Fall. He was not going to take any superficial surrender. He put His finger on each part of my self-life, and I had to decide to surrender it in cold blood. He could never take a thing away until I gave my consent. Then the moment I gave it, some purging took place (Isaiah 6:5-7).

"Woe to me!" I cried. "I am ruined! For I am a man of unclean lips, and I live among a people of unclean lips, and my eyes have seen the King, the Lord Almighty." Then one of the seraphim flew to me with a live coal in his hand, which he had taken with tongs from the altar. With it he touched my mouth and said, "See, this has touched your lips; your guilt is taken away and your sin atoned for."

I could never touch that thing again. It was not saying I was purged and the thing was still having a hold on me: no, it was a breaking, and the Holy Ghost taking control. Day by day the dealing went on. He was coming in as God, and I had lived as man, and *"what is permissible to an ordinary man,"* He told me, *"will not be permissible to you."*

You may feel there is no need for you to go down this route of total surrender to the Person of the Holy Spirit since that may be the reserve of those called to the ministry. But think again. Called or not called, we are all going to the same heaven as believers. We are all going to stand before the Judgment Seat of Christ as believers. We are all given the option to be the Bride of Christ, rather than just wedding guests like the wise virgins. To qualify, the Bride has to make herself ready.

If we are going to heaven because we have been washed in the Blood of the Lamb, why settle for a mediocre existence? Why not pay the price and be among those who will go with the Lamb wherever He goes. I believe life, as God intended it, actually starts after death: at the resurrection of the body.

The process can begin for you and me here and now when Jesus says to us: "*I know My sheep*" (John 10:14). He knows you.

Chapter Six
THE FIRE OF RESTORATION

John 21:6-15: He said, "Throw your net on the right side of the boat and you will find some." When they did, they were unable to haul the net in because of the large number of fish. Then the disciple whom Jesus loved said to Peter, "It is the Lord!" As soon as Simon Peter heard him say, "It is the Lord," he wrapped his outer garment round him (for he had taken it off) and jumped into the water. The other disciples followed in the boat, towing the net full of fish, for they were not far from shore, about a hundred metres. When they landed, they saw a fire of burning coals there with fish on it, and some bread. Jesus said to them, "Bring some of the fish you have just caught." So Simon Peter climbed back into the boat and dragged the net ashore. It was full of large fish, 153, but even with so many the net was not torn. Jesus said to them, "Come and have breakfast." None of the disciples dared ask him, "Who are you?" They knew it was the Lord. Jesus came, took the bread and gave it to them, and did the same with the fish. This was now the third time Jesus appeared to his disciples after he was raised from the dead. When they had finished eating, Jesus said to Simon Peter, "Simon son of John, do you love me more than these?" "Yes, Lord," he said, "you know that I love you." Jesus said, "Feed my lambs."

This is one of the most moving episodes in the Bible: the restoration of Peter. The fire on the beach served a dual purpose for Peter. None of the other disciples would have read any meaning into the fire lit by Jesus as He waited for the disciples to finish fishing. Peter, however, saw the double meaning straight away. Though the disciples had "toiled all night and caught nothing" Jesus had produced some miracle fish.

Here by the shore of the lake Jesus did one of his creative miracles. He had fish on a grill when no fish had been caught. He could also appear to the disciples wearing different clothes. He certainly didn't appear wearing his grave clothes because they were abandoned in the tomb.

So, when Peter saw the fire and the fish, he was convinced it was indeed the Lord. To the glory of God Jesus has not changed. He is the same yesterday, today and forever (Hebrews 13:8). He is still in the business of surprising us with His amazing and unique miracles, even when our faith is weak.

Jesus Loves to Do Extraordinary Miracles

There are miracles Jesus performs in answer to specific prayers requests; great miracles that often astound us, for He did promise:

Very truly I tell you, whoever believes in me will do the works I have been doing, and they will do even greater things than these, because I am going to the Father. And I will do whatever you ask in my name, so that the Father may be glorified in the Son. You may ask me for anything in my name, and I will do it (John 14:12-14).

This is where faith and divine activity work hand in hand. The person believing can do the works Jesus did because He has gone to the Father. With the miracle of the grilled fish on the lake shore, what Peter and the other disciples witnessed was Jesus performing a miracle nobody asked for. This miracle was all the more remarkable because without exception all the disciples had given up hope. Once Jesus died on the Cross, even with rumours of His rising from the dead, the disciples had no hope of a future. Now they were at a loose end. Some of them decided to follow Peter to do some fishing.

Now to him who is able to do immeasurably more than all we ask or imagine, according to his power that is at work within us... (Ephesians 3:20)

The fish on the grill was an unexpected and unsolicited miracle. It shows that God does not need us to pray before He can carry out His agenda, even concerning us.

The Second Fire Was Too Much

No doubt, this fire reminded Peter of the last time he stood by another fire in the High Priest's courtyard. How could he forget? It was there he made the greatest blunder of his life, when in spite of all his protestation and promises, Peter denied ever knowing Christ. Now it was a day of reckoning. Jesus had risen again, just as He said he would. Peter was left with not an ounce of integrity or self-respect.

He most definitely must have looked again into *that Face*. He would have expected a sharp reminder or rebuke from Jesus. Instead, the look on the face of the risen Lord would be full of compassion for Peter. Yes, Peter had flopped; he had disappointed even himself by his behaviour. The point, however, of the Cross is that God knows all about our faults and failings even before we have sinned. Because of the cross, He has made provision for our forgiveness and cleansing.

At the first fire Peter was looking into the face of the Teacher (Rabbi). Now he was looking into the face of the Saviour. It was the sinful nature of people like Peter that took Jesus to the Cross where He paid the price for our redemption.

Chapter Seven
THE GREAT TRANSACTION IS DONE

The Cross is a great eraser. Jesus and Peter were now looking at each other—face to face. Neither mentioned anything about Peter's past failures. Peter knew Jesus was the same Person. Yes, He had died and risen again, but His memory was intact. There was no chance of amnesia here. Yet, Jesus said 'not a word' to Peter about it.

Lessons to Learn from This Encounter

The last time Peter put his foot in it, Jesus rebuked him harshly, and in public.

Matthew 16:21-23 says, *From that time on Jesus began to explain to his disciples that he must go to Jerusalem and suffer many things at the hands of the elders, the chief priests and the teachers of the law, and that he must be killed and on the third day be raised to life. Peter took him aside and began to rebuke him. "Never, Lord!" he said. "This shall never happen to you!" Jesus turned and said to Peter, "Get behind me, Satan! You are a stumbling-block to me; you do not have in mind the concerns of God, but merely human concerns."*

Jesus had called some people many names that were not complimentary, especially the Pharisees. Not often, if ever, had He called someone "Satan." Yet, that is what He called Peter as if here Peter was a direct mouthpiece of the Great Dragon. How did Peter feel, I wonder?

In the same chapter of Matthew (verses 17-19) Jesus had given Peter the highest accolade ever.

Jesus replied, "Blessed are you, Simon son of Jonah, for this was not revealed to you by flesh and blood, but by my Father in heaven. And I tell you that you are Peter, and on this rock I will build my church, and the gates of Hades will not overcome it. I will give you the keys of the kingdom of heaven; whatever you bind on earth will be bound in heaven, and whatever you loose on earth will be loosed in heaven."

Now in a 360° turn around Peter was receiving the sharpest rebuke possible! Jesus was actually saying to Peter: "Get out of My way; what you are saying is from the enemy."

So, if for just saying what he thought about the need for the Cross, Peter received such a sharp rebuke, I wonder what might be going through Peter's head at that time. He had actually publicly denied Jesus. Just one step behind Judas who betrayed Him. The last person he wanted to ever face was Jesus, but there they were, face to face by the fire. Jesus, however, did not mention the denial.

The Cross made the difference. The sins and weaknesses of Peter have now been covered. Jesus had taken them all upon Himself. Peter was already broken enough.

A bruised reed he will not break, and a smouldering wick he will not snuff out" (Isaiah 42:3).

Jesus would never rub it in once a man has owned up to his failings as Peter had done.

Peter Is Moved Up to the Next Level

Peter had learnt a big lesson. He didn't have to be strong to win the race. He didn't have to outshine the rest of the apostles or to be a favourite. All Jesus wanted was for Peter to find his strength in Him. Now that he had learnt that lesson, he could be trusted with great responsibilities both to the world and to the rest of the disciples.

Being weak is a state we all find very difficult to handle, especially me. What I find most difficult about it is when the Holy Spirit expects you to be weak and to stay weak. It is all the harder to swallow when that weakness is a matter of choice. You don't have to be weak, but you choose to be weak so that the power of God may manifest through you.

It is easy now to see why Peter and the other disciples in the Upper Room were primed and ready for the Day of Pentecost. So much preparation had gone on before. By the time of the third fire, when tongues of fire fell on the 120, Peter in particular was totally empty of self, drained of self-sufficiency, and ready to accommodate whatever lifestyle the Holy Spirit chose to live through him.

Taking a Leaf from Paul's Book

Even if I should choose to boast, I would not be a fool, because I would be speaking the truth. But I refrain, so no one will think more of me than is warranted by what I do or say, or because of these surpassingly great revelations. Therefore, in order to keep me from becoming conceited, I was given a thorn in my flesh, a messenger of Satan, to torment me. Three times I pleaded with the Lord to take it away from me.
But he said to me, "My grace is sufficient for you, for my power is made perfect in weakness."
Therefore I will boast all the more gladly about my weaknesses, so that Christ's power may rest on me. That is why, for Christ's sake, I delight in weaknesses, in insults, in hardships, in persecutions, in difficulties. For when I am weak, then I am strong" (2 Corinthians 12:6-10).

Weaknesses Paul Had in Mind Here

Paul summarizes the weaknesses in four other words in verse 10: insults, hardships, persecutions, and calamities.

Insults: This is when people think of clever ways of making your faith or your lifestyle or your words look stupid or weird or inconsistent.

Hardships: circumstances forced upon you, reversals of fortune against your will. This could refer to any situation where you feel trapped. You didn't plan it or think it would be this way, but there you are, and it's hard.

Persecutions: wounds or abuses or painful circumstances or acts of prejudice or exploitation from people because of your Christian faith or your Christian moral commitments. It's when you are not treated fairly. You get a raw deal.

Calamities: (distresses, difficulties, or troubles) the idea is one of pressure or crushing or being weighed down; circumstances that tend to overcome you with stress and tension.

What These Weaknesses Are

These are the circumstances and situations and experiences and wounds that make us look weak;

things we would probably get rid of if we had the human strength. If we were "strong," we might return the insult with such an effective put down that the opponent would wither, and everyone would admire our wit and cleverness. If we were "strong" we might take charge of our own fortune and turn back the emerging hardship and change circumstances so that they go the way we want them to and not force us into discomfort. If we were "strong" we might turn back the persecution so quickly and so decisively that no one would mess with us again. If we were "strong" we might use our resources to get out of the calamity or distress as fast as possible or take charge of the situation and marshal our own resources so masterfully as to minimize its pressure.

In reality, we don't usually have that kind of human strength, and even when we may have it, as Christians, we don't use it the way the world does. Jesus tells us not to return evil for evil. Paul wrote,

When we are reviled, we bless; when we are persecuted, we endure; when we are slandered, we try to conciliate; we have become as the scum of the world, the dregs of all things (1 Corinthians 4:12-13 NASB).

In other words, this kind of lifestyle, this kind of response to abuse, looks weak and beggarly, feeble, anaemic, and inept—at least it looks that way to those who thrive on pride and equate power with the best come back.

So, our weaknesses are experiences, situations, circumstances, and wounds that are hard to bear and that we can't remove either because they are beyond our control or because love dictates that we do not return evil for evil. These experiences are not gained in an instance. Most likely they may be triggered in a meeting where the Holy Spirit is clearly at work, but the work is not done there. It is after the meeting or church service when the individual goes home to reflect and to seek the Lord deeper that the real work of grace begins. It was my custom as a young Christian to attend meetings to hear from God, but to go back home to meet with God.

I used to observe in my Bible College days when a powerful preacher came to speak to us nearly all of the student body might be moved to tears or remorse or other forms of contrition. After dismissal, as soon as we were outside the hall, many of my fellow students would laugh and joke as if they had never been touched by the Holy Spirit just less than five minutes before. Fortunately, I didn't form any close friendship with anybody that might have pulled me into mundane conversation or a change of topic.

I used to go straight to my room and on my knees, hoping that my roommate would just leave me alone with God. I could be there pleading with the Lord to meet with me so that the message would have a lasting impact on me. Over the years since then, I have observed that students who went that extra mile in really meeting with the Lord late into the night went on to do exploits for the Lord at home and abroad. A name that stands out is Reinhard Bonnke, who attended the same Bible College.

Chapter Eight
THE COMING OF THE HOLY SPIRIT

Acts 2:1-4 says, *When the day of Pentecost came, they were all together in one place. Suddenly a sound like the blowing of a violent wind came from heaven and filled the whole house where they were sitting. They saw what seemed to be tongues of fire that separated and came to rest on each of them. All of them were filled with the Holy Spirit and began to speak in other tongues as the Spirit enabled them.*

We have seen what happened to Peter by the first fire: he had a revelation of his self-life. He realised with a bitter experience that after all these years he didn't know himself as he thought. It was a shock to his system that after all his self- confidence and bold confession of his devotion and loyalty to Christ, at the last hurdle he flopped. He denied knowing Christ— and not just once, not twice, but three times.

When Peter denied Christ, he wasn't under any delusion. He knew what he was doing. His problem had its root in what God showed him. If Jesus is the Christ, the Son of the living God, then how could He die? How could the One proclaiming the coming of the Kingdom of Heaven end it all on the cross like a common criminal? When Peter saw that Jesus didn't resist arrest, he didn't call on the angels to rescue him, and he didn't transfigure and dazzle his enemies as He did on the Mount of Transfiguration, Peter had a breakdown. He denied knowing Jesus because this ending was not what he had signed up for and what he was expecting.

What had dawned on Peter after the cock crowed and made him to cry bitterly was how shallow his own commitment was. Just because you don't understand what God is doing is no excuse to turn away from what you have believed all your life.

The question some of us need to ask ourselves from time to time is: if there was no heaven to gain, would I still follow Christ and devote my time and energy serving Him? Would I believe in God if He wasn't there for me when I needed Him? This is the type of questions young people often ask. They want to see a tangible benefit for serving Christ. It is like He owes them an explanation. He must prove Himself worthy of their allegiance.

One of the young men in one of our churches lost his dad. The man was a devoted father and a pillar in the church. He had cancer and the church prayed and believed he would recover. The young man believed God is a good God and He would not allow his father to pass away before his time. But the father died. The young man lost his faith. He stopped coming to church. His reasoning was: "What is the point in praying if God is going to do what He wants anyway." Unfortunately, he is not alone in demanding God prove Himself in order to command their allegiance.

Paris Reidhead's Perspective

"Dear friends, there's only one reason, one reason, for a sinner to repent. That's because Jesus Christ deserves the worship and the adoration and the love and the obedience of his heart. Not because he'll go to heaven. If the only reason you repented, dear friend, was to keep out of Hell, you're trying to serve God because He'll do you good! But a repentant heart is a heart that has seen something of the enormity of the crime of playing God and denying the just and righteous God the worship and obedience that He deserves!"

"Why should a sinner repent? Because God deserves the obedience and love that the sinner has refused to give Him. Not so that he'll go to heaven. If the only reason he repents is so that he'll go to heaven, it's nothing but trying to make a deal or a bargain with God."

"Why should a sinner give up all his sins? Why should he be challenged to do it? Why should he make restitution when he's coming to Christ? Because God deserves the obedience that He demands."

I have talked with people who have no assurance that their sins are forgiven. They want to feel safe before they're willing to commit themselves to Christ.

But I believe that the only ones whom God actually witnesses by His Spirit are born of Him are the people who come to Jesus Christ and say something like this: "Lord Jesus, I'm going to obey You, and love You, and serve You, and do what You want me to do as long as I live, even if I get nothing out of it, simply because You are worthy to be loved, and obeyed, and served, and I'm not trying to make a deal with You!"

The statement above: "Lord Jesus, I'm going to obey you, and love you, and serve you, and do what you want me to do, as long as I live, even if I get nothing at the end of it," is a hard pill to swallow for a committed Christian, much less an unbeliever. In modern day evangelism we try to entice unbelievers. We keep lowering the bar—or have no bar at all—in an effort to make it easy for the world to believe in Christ. "Come to Christ, and all your problems will be over, and you will have access to heaven as a bonus. If after three months you are not completely satisfied, you can stop believing and still get to keep all the special gifts." Then we wonder why so many "converts" fall away or remain weak and worldly."

Basically, an average sinner may look like an innocent, decent, family man, law-abiding and may even be a church goer. According to the Bible a sinner is not only defined by what he does, but also by what he is:

a) *Surely, I was sinful at birth, sinful from the time my mother conceived me* (Psalm 51:5 NIV).

b) *Everyone who sins breaks the law; in fact, sin is lawlessness.* (1 John 3:4 NIV)

c) *Therefore, anyone who chooses to be a friend of the world becomes an enemy of God.* (James 4:4 NIV)

d) *But his subjects hated him and sent a delegation after him to say, "We don't want this man to be our king"* (Luke 19:14 NIV)

e) Lastly, and more universally, Isaiah 53:2-3 lays bare the attitude of every sinner towards Jesus Christ. "*He had no beauty or majesty to attract us to him, nothing in his appearance that we should desire him. He was despised and rejected by mankind, a man of suffering, and familiar with pain.*"

Chapter Nine
CHECK THE SOIL

Here is our problem: Up to ninety percent of the evangelistic crop is failing; they wither and die as soon as the sunlight of tribulation, persecution, and temptation shines on them. We encourage them to be watered by the Word. We give them the "fertilizer" of counsel and support. We follow them up thoroughly, but all to no avail.

So, we then need to check the soil. If, before we plant the seed of the gospel, we take the time to thoroughly turn the soil of the heart with the Law, the effect will be the removal of the stones of sin upon repentance. God has given us insight into the area in which we are planting. The ground of the human heart is very hard. The Scriptures call it a *"heart of stone"* (Ezekiel 36:26).

I have heard a number of well-known preachers say that it is a biblical norm to have seventy-five percent of those coming to Christ fall away. During an altar call, they know that only one in four of those responding to their message will continue in their faith. So, more than likely they are not too alarmed by modern statistics that reveal an eighty to ninety percent failure.

This thought is based on the Parable of the Sower, which shows that only twenty-five percent of the crop was on good soil (Mark 4:1–20). But I don't think Jesus gave us this parable as a consolation for disappointing evangelistic results. I think He gave it for our instruction.

When we study the parable closely, we see that the good-soil hearer, the *genuine* convert, had some things the other hearers didn't have. He had *understanding* (Matthew 13:23), and he had a *noble and good heart* (Luke 8:15). Does that mean that throughout humanity, there are those who somehow have understanding and a noble and good heart, and we have to keep on sowing until we find them? No, Scripture makes it clear that there is *none* who understands (Romans 3:11), and that the heart of man is not good, but deceitful and desperately wicked (Jeremiah 17:9).

These statistics of an eighty-four to ninety-seven percent fall-away rate are not confined to crusades but are general throughout local church evangelism. In his book *Fresh Wind, Fresh Fire*, Jim Cymbala notes the lack of growth in the Church:

> Despite all the Christian broadcasting and high-profile campaigns, the Christian population is not growing in numbers nationally. In fact, church attendance in a given week during 1996 was down to 37 percent of the population, a ten-year low . . . even though 82 percent of Americans claim to be Christians.

The problem is not with the crusades, but with the methods and message of modern evangelism. A preacher was in a dilemma. He was preaching the light of the gospel (Christ's death, burial, and resurrection) without using the Law to awaken his hearers. Like many others who see this enigma, he thought that his converts needed more follow-up.

A respected minister, whose evangelism programme has exploded across the world, said that his policy attempts to get at the heart of the fall-away rate of new converts "by placing great stress on the follow-up." However, to fall into the trap of thinking that follow-up is the answer is like supposing that putting a stillborn child into intensive care will solve the problem.

A senior minister of a large growing church noticed a new situation in their church. An increasing number of converts were bringing their old ways into their Christian lives and doing things that shocked their leaders. The first thing to note is that this church and its ministers haven't diluted the gospel or lowered their standards. The church is one of the best in the country with gifted, godly leaders. They fearlessly preach a no-compromise gospel and are even better at nurture than they were years ago. Yet an increasing number of their numerous converts fail to show evidence of moral change in their lives.

In a 1990 crusade in the U.S., 600 decisions were obtained. No doubt there was much rejoicing. However, ninety days later, follow-up workers *couldn't find even one* who was continuing in his or her faith. That crusade created 600 "backsliders," or to be more scriptural, "false converts." In Cleveland, Ohio, in an "Inner City Outreach," rejoicing no doubt tapered when those who were involved in follow-up once again couldn't find one of the 400 who had made a decision.

In 1985, a four-day crusade obtained 217 decisions, but according to a member of the organizing committee, ninety-two percent fell away. Charles E. Hackett, the Division of Home Missions National Director for the Assemblies of God in the U.S., said, "A soul at the altar does not generate much excitement in some circles because we realize approximately ninety-five out of every hundred will not become integrated into the church. In fact, most of them will not return for a second visit." A pastor in Boulder, Colorado, sent a team to Russia in 1991 and attained 2,500 decisions. The next year, they found that only 30 were going on in their faith. That's a little more than a one-percent retention rate. In Leeds, England, a visiting U.S. speaker acquired 400 decisions for a local church. However, six weeks later only two were going on, and they eventually fell away.

A leading U.S. denomination published that during 1995 they secured 384,057 decisions but retained only 22,983 in fellowship. They couldn't account for 361,074 supposed conversions. That's a ninety-four percent fall-away rate. Pastor Dennis Grenell from Auckland, New Zealand, who has travelled to India every year since 1980, reported that he saw 80,000 decision cards stacked in a hut in the city of Rajamundry, the "results" of past evangelistic crusades. But he maintained that one would be fortunate to find even 80 Christians in the entire city.

Even a "no-compromise gospel" will not awaken sinners. That's not its function. Author and Bible teacher Paris Reidhead, in remarking about the ministry of Charles Finney, wrote:

> Finney was in Rochester, New York, where a blue-ribbon committee of outstanding citizens was appointed by Henry Ward Beecher to study the converts who, a decade earlier, had come to Christ under Finney's preaching. It was found that eighty-five percent of those who had made professions of faith under Finney's preaching were still faithfully living for Christ. In contrast, it is being reported that only one-half of one percent of those who make decisions for Christ in our evangelistic meetings today will be living as Christians two years from now. This should give you some idea of how far we've strayed from the Word of God.

Please, don't be tempted to ignore the devastating results of modern evangelism, and to look at those *comparatively* few who are continuing in their faith as justification for the method. Remember, for every 1,000 genuine converts, there are as many as 9,000 who lay mangled on the soil of hard hearts, as a direct result of the quick and easy methods of modern evangelism.

What Did Jesus Do When
He Confronted a Sinner?

He made the issue one of righteousness rather than happiness. He used the Ten Commandments to show sinners the righteous standard of God. In Mark 10:17, a man came running to Jesus, knelt before Him, and asked how he could obtain everlasting life. This man came "running." He "knelt" before the Saviour. It would seem that his earnest and humble heart made him a prime candidate as a potential convert. Yet Jesus didn't give him the message of God's grace. He didn't even mention the love of God. Neither did He tell him of an abundant, wonderful new life. Instead, He used the Law of God to expose his hidden sin. This man was a transgressor of the First of the Ten Commandments. His money was his god, and you cannot serve both God and money. Then the Scriptures reveal that it was *love* that motivated Jesus to speak in this way to this rich young man (Mark 10:21). Every time we witness to someone, we should challenge our motives. Do we love the sinner enough to make sure his conversion is genuine; or do we love the feeling of getting another decision for Jesus— when in truth our zeal without knowledge has just produced another potential Judas?

Why did Jesus take the time to use the Ten Commandments? His method seems a little archaic compared to the quick and easy instant converts of modern methods.

Dr Martyn Lloyd-Jones gives us the answer

A gospel which merely says, "Come to Jesus," and offers Him as a Friend and offers a marvellous new life without convincing of sin is not New Testament evangelism. (The essence of evangelism is to start by preaching the Law; and it is because the Law has not been preached that we have had so much superficial evangelism.) True evangelism... must always start by preaching the Law. When you use the Law (the Ten Commandments) to show the world their true state, get ready for them to thank you. For the first time in their lives, they will see the Christian message as an expression of love and concern for their eternal welfare rather than of merely proselytizing for a better lifestyle while on this earth. They begin to understand why they should be *concerned* about their eternal salvation. The Law shows them that they are condemned by God. It even makes them a little fearful.

Perhaps you are tempted to say that we should *never* condemn sinners. However, Scripture tells us that they are *already* condemned (John 3:18). All the Law does is show them their true state. If you dust a table in your living room and think it is dust-free, try pulling back the curtains and letting in the early morning sunlight. You will more than likely see dust still sitting on the table. The sunlight didn't create the dust, *it merely exposed it*. When we take the time to draw back the high and heavy curtains of the Holy of

Holies and let the light of God's Law shine upon the sinner's heart, all that happens is that the Law shows him his true state before God. Proverbs 6:23 tells us that "the Commandment is a lamp, and the Law is light."

Chapter Ten
PETER WAS SIFTED LIKE WHEAT

Simon, Simon, Satan has asked to sift all of you as wheat. But I have prayed for you, Simon, that your faith may not fail. And when you have turned back, strengthen your brothers (Luke 22:31).

Without the first fire in the High Priest's courtyard where Peter had his revelation of his self-life, the tongues of fire falling upon him on the day of Pentecost would have made a limited impact. Peter would have experienced no more than the average Pentecostal/Charismatic Christian today. Speaking in tongues and raising the arms in worship are perhaps what he would have experienced.

You cannot be filled without first being empty. You cannot sow seeds in the soil until you had first broken up the fallow ground. People often cry out, "More of You, Lord," whereas they should be yelling at the top of their lungs, "Less of me, Lord." If I don't decrease, He cannot increase. Being filled with the Holy Spirit is relatively simple and easy. Just make sure you are empty.

Not Everything Happens by Prayer

Life for the believer would be ten times less complicated—and certainly less painful—if only all the changes that need to take place in our lives can be fixed on our knees. There is the cross to carry, daily, for example. We are supposed to hang on the cross, and not for the cross to hand around our neck as a fashion statement. Carrying your cross and waiting for someone else to nail you on it is no joke. It can be painful and humiliating.

So, Satan had targeted the Twelve. Eleven of them he wanted to tempt to the maximum. One of them, Judas, he wanted to destroy, since he had been a collaborator. To Judas, Jesus just let him know that He was aware of his dastardly deeds. "Whatever you do," Jesus urged Judas, "do it quickly" (John 13:27).

The resolve of the rest of the apostles to stand firm and follow Jesus all the way to the bitter end was going to be severely tested. Indeed, they were tested. Jesus prayed, but He didn't pray for them all; and He didn't pray for them to be spared the testing. They were left open to the enemy attack because each of them needed to discover that when it came to crunch time that the flesh would let them down. It is amazing how so few of us, especially among the ministers of God, know that the flesh is weak.

Matthew 26:40-41 says, *Then he returned to his disciples and found them sleeping. "Couldn't you men keep watch with me for one hour?" he asked Peter. "Watch and pray so that you will not fall into temptation. The spirit is willing, but the flesh is weak."*

No, Jesus didn't pray that the apostles would be delivered from the attack of Satan. He didn't pray for them at all. The only prayer He prayed at this time was for Peter, and it was not to stop the attack either. *"I have prayed for you, Simon, that your faith may not fail."* Jesus prayed for resilience for Peter: that though he may fail, he would not fall. Until you become aware of the total depravity of the flesh, the Adamic fallen nature, you can never be an instrument in the hands of God.

God is looking for a chance to show each and everyone of us that we are corrupt to the core. Paul discovered this truth, and it led him to become one of the greatest apostles that has ever lived. He said in Romans 7:23,

I know that good itself does not dwell in me, that is, in my sinful nature. For I have the desire to do what is good, but I cannot carry it out.

The bad news is that not many believers know this truth about themselves. So, they try hard to improve and to change. The second bad news is: you cannot change, so give up trying and listen to what the Spirit is saying to the churches.

Luke 18:18-19: *A certain ruler asked him, "Good teacher, what must I do to inherit eternal life?" "Why do you call me good?" Jesus answered. "No one is good—except God alone."*

Matthew 7:9-11: *Which of you, if your son asks for bread, will give him a stone? Or if he asks for a fish, will give him a snake? If you, then, though you are evil, know how to give good gifts to your children, how much more will your Father in heaven give good gifts to those who ask him!*

The first of these texts is self-explanatory, but the point I am raising is doubly explicit in the second text. Firstly, we know Jesus is addressing believers. He said, *'how much more will your Father in heaven"*; and so clarifying who He was addressing. Secondly, He states: *"If you, then, though you are evil..."* That was Jesus' verdict on the human nature. It is corrupt and it cannot change. Although at conversion it is declared justified, it still remains in itself evil.

When we confess our sins, repent, and believe in Christ, our sins are covered, forgiven. We will never face God as Judge but as Justifier and Father. What justification deals with is our guilt, our relationship with God. We are now reconciled; the middle wall of partition has been removed, but it doesn't change our nature. I still remain bound to my root in the Adamic nature.

My Flesh Remains Flesh

The flesh can never become divine. The only hope you and I have is become partakers.

2 Peter 1:4-5 says, *His divine power has given us everything we need for a godly life through our knowledge of him who called us by his own glory and goodness. Through these he has given us his very great and precious promises, so that through them you may participate in the divine nature, having escaped the corruption in the world caused by evil desires.*

I participate in the divine nature. In other words, it is only possible for me to live like God if the Holy Spirit lives His life through me. For Him to live through me, therefore, I must be totally at His disposal. If He is not Lord of all, He is not Lord at all. This is the hidden formula behind the statement: be filled with the Holy Spirit.

Speaking in tongues is the evidence that the Holy Spirit has come in. It is not a sign that He is in full control. The Holy Spirit is not a liquid; He is not a putty you apply to fill cracks. He is a Person. When He comes into our lives He comes in as God. He has not come to live our lives, but to live the life of Jesus Christ through us. He won't even start to do that until we get out of His way.

That getting out of the way was the reason Jesus didn't pray for Peter to be spared the trauma of the denial. He prayed rather that his faith would not fail. Peter needed to learn something about himself: he is not strong until the Holy Spirit becomes his strength. *"For in him we live and move and have our being"* (Acts 17:28).

The Mystery of God's Way

The way Jesus handled the support He promised the apostles during this coming crisis reveals how God uses delegation as an essential tool. Satan targeted the Twelve in his attacks, but Jesus prayed only for one of them: Peter. It goes to show the value God places upon the human agency. God often works directly to bring solution and deliverance in a situation. In other times, however, He does it through men.

> *Simon, Simon, Satan has asked to sift all of you as wheat. But I have prayed for you, Simon, that your faith may not fail. And when you have turned back, strengthen your brothers* (Luke 22:31).

Satan is to sift "all of you." *"But I have prayed for you, Simon,"* Jesus said. Why did Satan attack all the apostles, but Jesus only prayed for Peter? Having faced the ordeal and failed spectacularly, and then to be restored by the lake shore, Peter was well placed to take on the task of strengthening the brethren.

Peter would need to take his time to re-educate his fellow apostles that it was ok to be weak; not to try to draw upon their strength which will ultimately fail again, but to let the Holy Spirit take the strain. No one was more qualified for the job than Peter.

Chapter Eleven
WHEN HE COMES, HE WILL CONVICT

Jesus, speaking about the Holy Spirit, said in John 16:8, *"When he comes, he will prove the world to be in the wrong about sin and righteousness and judgment."*

The whole point of having a personal revival is not only its effect on our personal lives, but on the world of unbelievers around us. This is particularly crucial in the work of the ministry. Without the convicting power of the Holy Spirit accompanying our preaching or witnessing, the sinner will not be moved. No doubt there are various ways and means of attracting people to church; all very necessary and commendable. However, we will never win the sinner to Christ without him repenting, otherwise the conversion experience will be shallow, or even false.

Acts 2:36-38 declares, *"Therefore let all Israel be assured of this: God has made this Jesus, whom you crucified, both Lord and Messiah." When the people heard this, they were cut to the heart and said to Peter and the other apostles, "Brothers, what shall we do?" Peter replied, "Repent and be baptized, every one of you, in the name of Jesus Christ for the forgiveness of your sins. And you will receive the gift of the Holy Spirit."*

When Peter preached the gospel, the people were "cut to the heart." They were gripped by the convicting and irresistible power of the Holy Spirit. In other words, Peter's hearers were made aware of their dire and dangerous state as sinners in the hands of an angry God. Without this assistance from the Holy Spirit, no preacher can expect to lead a soul to Christ unless he dilutes the message. For if there is no repentance toward God, there can be no faith in Jesus Christ.

What Rev Duncan Campbell had to say:

(The man who led the revival in the Hebrides, Scotland 1949-53)

"Today, we have a Christianity made easy as an accommodation to an age that is unwilling to face the implication of Calvary, and the gospel of "simply believism" has produced a harvest of professions which have done untold harm to the cause of Christ. How easy it is to live more or less in the enjoyment of God's free grace, and yet not realize that we are called to fulfil a divinely appointed purpose. There is a kind of gospel being proclaimed today which conveniently accommodates itself to the spirit of the age and makes no demand for godliness."

To me, one of the most disturbing features of present-day evangelism is the overemphasis on what man can do, and I believe this to be the reason why we so often fail to get men and women to make the contact with Christ which is so vital. The average man is not going to be impressed by our publicity, our posters, or our programmes, but let there be a demonstration of the supernatural in the realm of religion, and at once man is arrested.

I am disturbed by the attitude of the Church in general toward aggressive evangelism or revival. By evangelism I do not mean just an effort to get people back into the Church; this effort, while commendable, does not get us very far. What I mean is something much more: it is the getting of men and women into vital, saving and covenant relationship with Jesus Christ, and to be so supernaturally altered that holiness will characterize their whole being: body, soul, and spirit. It seems to me that the time has surely come when we must, with open mind and true heart, face ourselves with unqualified honesty and ask the question: "Am I alive to my responsibility as a labourer in God's vineyard?"

There is a power that is placed at the disposal of the Church that can out-manoeuvre and baffle the very strategy of Hell, and cause death and defeat to vanish before the presence of the Lord of Life. Yet, how is it that while we make such great claims for the power of the Gospel, we see so little of the supernatural in operation? Is there any reason why the Church today cannot everywhere equal the

Church at Pentecost? What did the early Church have that we do not possess today? Nothing but the Holy Spirit, nothing but the power of God. Here I would suggest that one of the main secrets of success in the early Church lay in the fact that the early believers believed in unction from on high and not entertainment from men. I think one of the keys to Pentecost was a 10-day prayer meeting with real repentance, fasting and unity.

One of the very sad features that characterizes much that goes under the name of evangelism today is the craze for entertainment. Here is an extract from a letter received from a leader in youth work in one of our great cities: "We are at our wits' end to know what to do with the young people who made a profession of conversion recently. They are demanding all sorts of entertainment, and it seems to us that if we fail to provide the entertainment that they want, we are not going to hold them."

Yes, the trend of the time in which we live is toward a Christian experience that is light and flippant and fed on entertainment. Some time ago, I listened to a young man give his testimony. He made a decision quite recently, and in giving his testimony this is what he said: "I have discovered that the Christian way of life can best be described, not as a battle, but as a song mingled with the sound of happy laughter." Far be it from me to move the song or happy laughter from religion, but I want to protest that that young man's conception was entirely wrong, and not in keeping with true New Testament Christianity.

"Oh, but," say the advocates of this way of thinking, "how are we to get the people if we do not provide some sort of entertainment?" To that I ask the question, how did they get the people at Pentecost? How did the early Church get the people? By publicity projects, by bills, by posters, by parades, by pictures? No! The people were arrested and drawn together and brought into vital relationship with God, not by sounds from men, but by sounds from heaven. We are in need of more sounds from heaven today."

The Apostles Were Ordinary Men

The Apostles were not men of influence—not many mighty, not many noble. The Master Himself did not choose to be a man of influence. "He made Himself of no reputation," which is to say that God chose power rather than influence. I sometimes think of Paul and Silas in Philippi. They had not enough influence to keep them out of prison but possessed the power of God in such a manner that their prayers in prison shook the whole prison to its very foundations. Not influence, but power.

I would to God that a wave of real godly fear gripped our land. This is what our age needs, not an easy-moving message, the sort of thing that makes the hearer feel all nice inside, but a message that is profoundly disturbing. We have been far too afraid of disturbing people, but the Holy Spirit will have nothing to do with a message or with a minister who is afraid of disturbing. Calvary was anything but nice to look at, blood-soaked beams of wood, a bruised and bleeding body, not nice to look upon. But then Jesus was not dealing with a nice thing. He was dealing with the sin of the world, and that is what we are called upon to deal with today. Jesus was made sin. Sin covered His wracked body.

The Early Church
Believed in the Supernatural

Someone has said that at Pentecost, God set the Church at Jerusalem on fire and the whole city came out to see it burn. I tell you if that happened in any church today, within hours the whole of the town would be out to see the burning, and they would be caught in the flames.

Revival is not going to come merely by attending conferences. When *"Zion travailed, she brought forth children."* Oh, may God bring us there, may God lead us through to the place of absolute surrender. Is it not true that our very best moments of yielding and consecration are mingled with the destructive element of self-preservation? A full and complete surrender is the price of blessing; it is the price of revival.

Conclusion

So, we have seen Peter on three fronts. At the first fire, he was strip-searched. At the second fire, he was restored. At Pentecost, he was set on fire of the Holy Spirit. For us today, as with Peter of old, all three stages are necessary for our spiritual journey. You can never finish a race you never started, and you cannot complete a course you did not begin. There is nothing more rewarding than to look back like Paul and have his testimony.

> *I have fought the good fight, I have finished the race, I have kept the faith. Now there is in store for me the crown of righteousness, which the Lord, the righteous Judge, will award to me on that day—and not only to me, but also to all who have longed for his appearing* (2 Timothy 4:7-8).

This is the essence of seeking first the Kingdom. It is the only offer on the table. For there is no seeking first the Kingdom, and subsequently seeing second the material things of this world. Not at all. The formula for being a success in life is: Godliness with contentment is great gain. If you can learn to be content, you gain the Kingdom and have everything else thrown in. You do the seeking; God does the adding.

May each one of us today experience each of these three fires.

About the Author

Rev. Dr. Paul Jinadu was born a Muslim in Lagos, Nigeria. He became a Christian after Jesus appeared to him, and he then abandoned his pursuit of a medical education in the United Kingdom. He went to The Bible College of Wales, Swansea in 1962 and later also studied theology at The London Bible College, where he graduated in 1972. He married Kate who he met in Bible College, and they returned to Nigeria as Missionaries in 1966. They first worked with the Apostolic Church in Lagos, and then extensively with the Foursquare Gospel Church as pastors and church planters.

They returned to the UK in the early 80's, with Paul going all over the country as a travelling evangelist and conference speaker. In 1985, at the invitation of many of his disciples, Paul started the New Covenant Church in Nigeria, and a year later in the UK. He now oversees hundreds of churches in around 50 nations of the world. Paul was the second President of the African and Caribbean Evangelical Alliance in the UK. He is an Apostle, spiritual father, and mentor to many pastors across the globe; a sought-after speaker and author of *I Have Seen the Lord* and many other books. He conducts leadership seminars and training all over the world.

For more information: www.nccworld.org